spiders

spiders

Sarah R. Riedman

An Easy-Read Fact Book

Franklin Watts
New York | London | Toronto | 1979

ACKNOWLEDGMENTS

The author is deeply indebted to two persons for reading the manuscript, for helpful comments and suggested changes, and especially for pointing out inaccuracies. Mr. George S. Fichter, entomologist, is the author and editor of numerous as well as diverse books in the broad field of natural science; Mr. Edwin L. Licht, arachnologist, active member of both the American and the British Arachnological Societies, is Museum Curator-Adjoint of Arachnology at the University of Colorado Museum in Boulder, Colorado, where he cares for arachnid collections and identifies spiders for medical and other interested persons.

Photographs courtesy of:
Walker Van Ripper Collection, University of Colorado Museum: pp. 5, 7, 11, 12, 13, 16, 18, 19, 21, 22, 24, 28, 29, 30, 31, 32, 33, 34, 42, 43, 44, 45, 46, 47;
William B. Love: pp. 10, 23, 29, 37, 39, 40, 41;
U.S.D.A.: pp. 6, 15, 17, 38;
NASA: pp. 20, 25, 26;
P. N. Witt: p. 27;
American Museum of Natural History: p. 35.

Art on p. 9 by Robert McGlynn.

Library of Congress Cataloging in Publication Data

Riedman, Sarah Regal, 1902-
Spiders.

(An Easy-read fact book)
Includes index.
SUMMARY: Describes the physical characteristics, habits, and natural environment of various types of spiders. I. Title.
QL458.4.R53 595′.44 79-1455
ISBN 0-531-02853-4

R.L. 2.5 Spache Revised Formula

Printed in the United Kingdom
6 5 4 3 2 1

A humpback garden spider in the center of its web.

Spiders are tiny creatures. Most of them can't hurt people. They seem afraid of people.

Only a few kinds live inside houses.

Most make their homes in fields and gardens.

They can be found in very dry, sandy places and in very damp places.

Some live in very warm places and others in very cold places.

There are spiders that live in caves or under the ground and even under water.

U.S.D.A.

A jumping spider

Spiders have got a bad name—which is not fair.
What are spiders really like?
They eat live food, mostly insects.
Few spiders bite people. None spread disease.
What is a spider?

A burrowing wolf spider and its next meal—
an insect.

Some people think a spider is a "strange kind of insect."

Not true.

Spiders have eight legs. Insects have six.

Insects have antennae. Spiders do not.

Spiders have two body parts. Insects have three.

Most insects have wings. Spiders do not have wings.

SPIDER

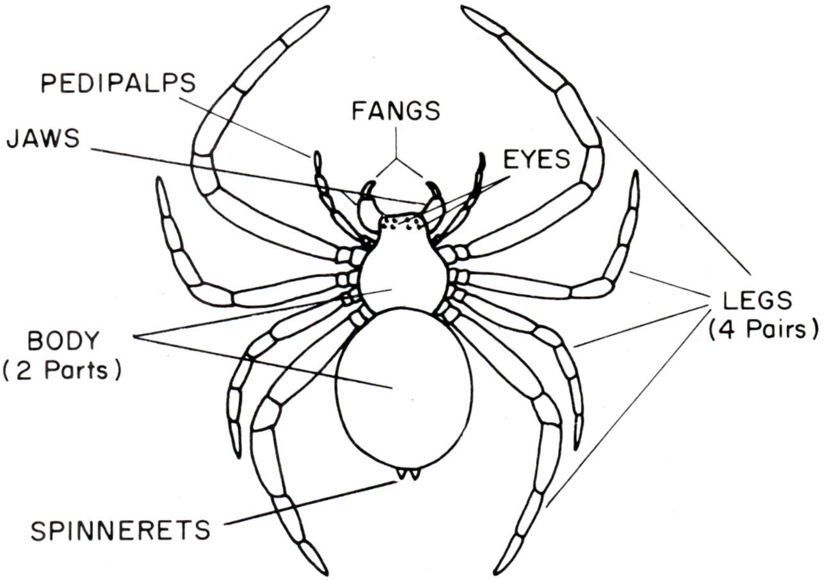

INSECT

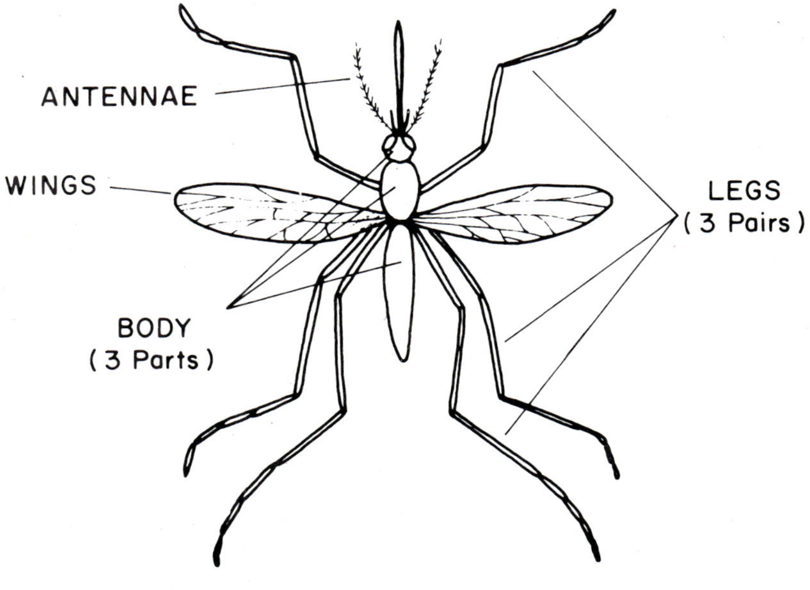

**Although they may not look alike,
this scorpion is closely related to the spider family.**

Spiders are ARACHNIDS (a-RACK-nedz). They belong to the family of ARTHROPODS (ar-throw-PODZ). Arthropods are animals that have jointed legs.

Other arachnids are scorpions, daddy longlegs, ticks, and mites.

But spiders are the only arachnids that spin silk.

The spider's eyes are set in many different ways.

Some spiders have six eyes and some have only four.

Most spiders do not see very well.

Even though this wolf spider has six eyes, like most spiders it doesn't see very well.

The spinnerets (spin-ne-RETZ) are the little tubes at the tip of the abdomen.

Each has a kind of faucet.

The spider has glands that spin silk.

The silk comes out through the spinnerets.

A black widow spider in her web.

A rare photograph of a tarantula guarding her egg sac.

The silk has many uses in the spider's life.

The silk web is a trap for catching insects.

The spider's egg sac is made of silk.

A spider uses a silk dragline to drop from the web to rest on a plant.

With a dragline a spider can leap into the air to catch an insect.

A dragline can be a track for a male to find a mate.

MEET A SPIDER FAMILY

Mother, father, and babies.
The ways of this family may surprise us.
The male and the female do not live together.

The female is much larger than the male.
She has a big abdomen (AB-dough-mun). His is small.
Her jaws are very, very strong. Her fangs are sharp.
Her glands make plenty of poison.
When the poison goes into an insect, it can't move.

Like most types of spiders, the female black widow (top) is larger than the male (bottom).

U.S.D.A.

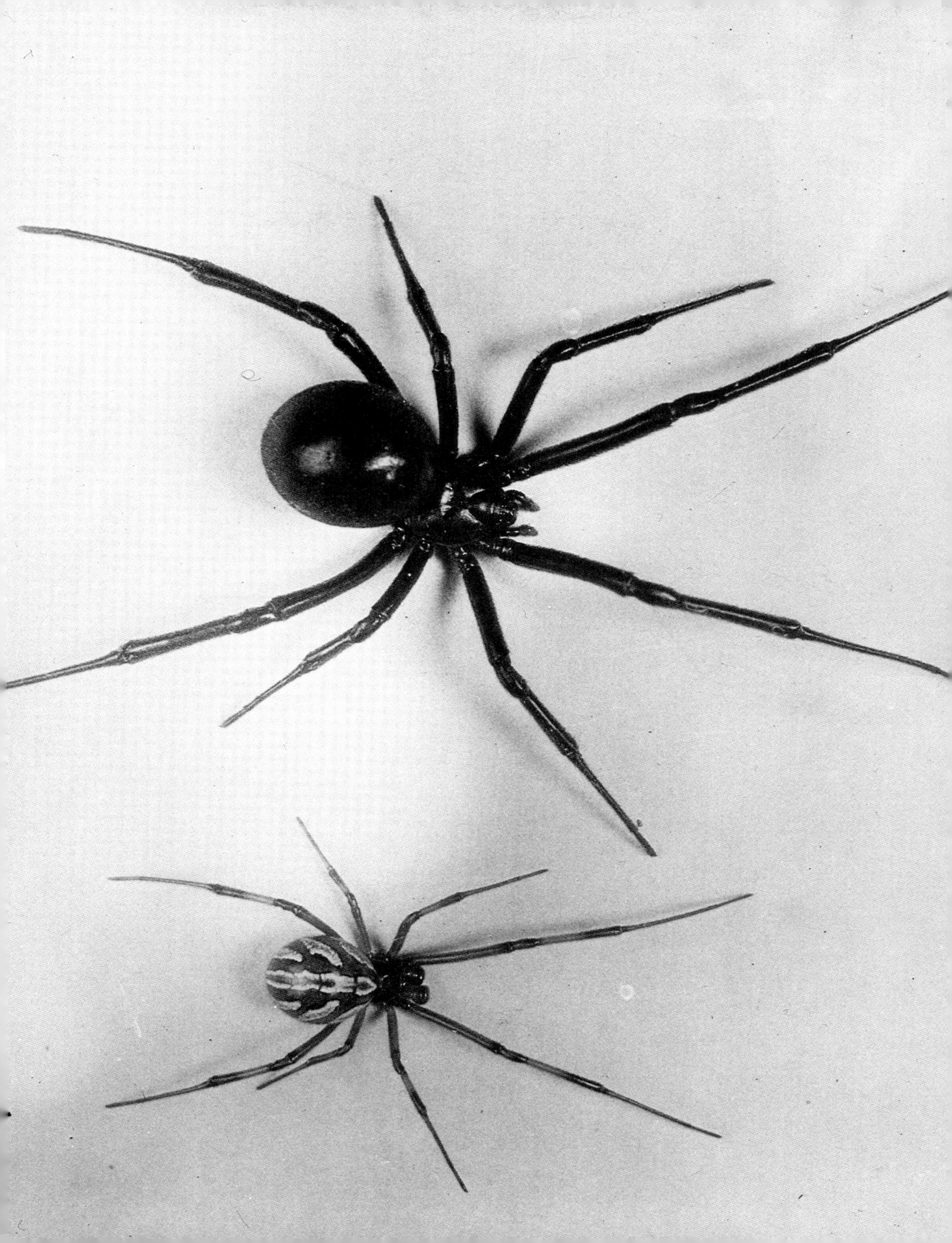

A female black widow

The female is a better spinner than the male.

She can fix the web when it seems it might come apart.

Her egg sac protects the eggs until they hatch.

U.S.D.A.

A black widow spider with red markings on its underside.

Most male spiders are tiny, but their legs are long.

A male spider is good-looking and brightly colored. His hair shines.

He does little or no weaving, and eats very little.

PLENTY OF SPIDERS

There are more than 30,000 different kinds of spiders in the world.

We know each family and kind by the way it does things. We know it by the way it gets its food, the way it builds a nest, and cares for its young.

Black widow babies, called spiderlings, coming out of their egg sac.

An orb-weaving spider with a grasshopper wrapped in its web.

THE SPINNERS

All spiders can spin, but only some build webs to trap their food.

One spider family weaves very beautiful webs. These spinners are the **orb weavers**.

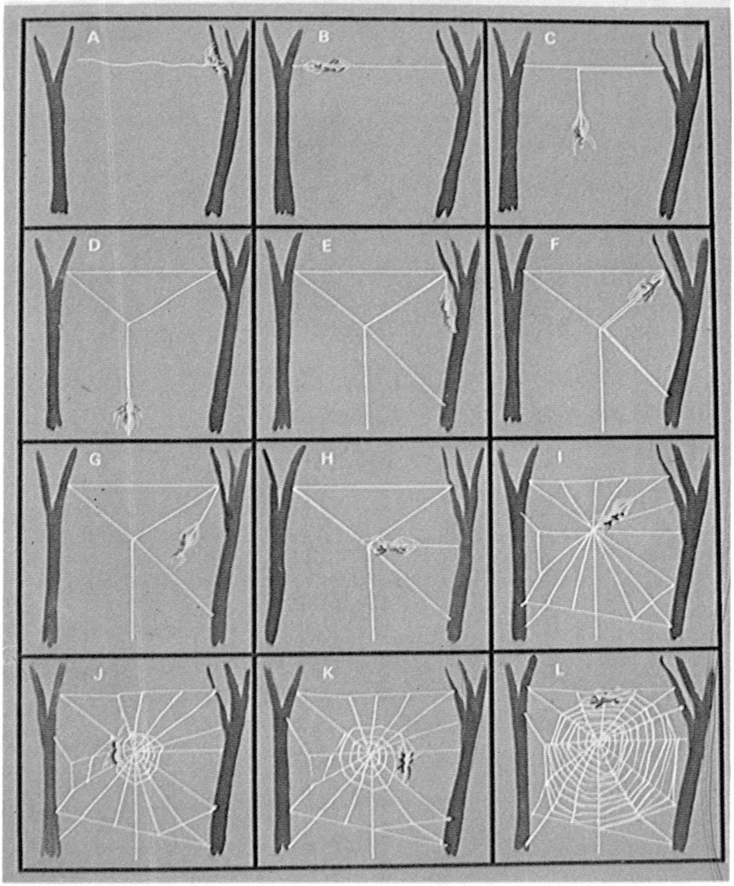

NASA

The many steps involved in weaving a web.

The spider stands on a branch, and lets its silk out in a stream.

This stream becomes hard. It is then a silk thread.

A light wind carries it to a neighboring branch.

The thread sticks there to make a bridge.

The spider continues the web until the job is done. Then she returns to the middle of the web.

She waits there to trap anything that comes by.

A black and yellow garden spider on its web.

Spiders are born knowing how to spin. Each kind makes a different kind of web.

She sits in the middle of the web, until suddenly she feels the silk threads moving.

An insect has come into her trap. It can't get out because the silk is sticky.

She jumps on the tiny insect.

Even a big, strong grasshopper that doesn't get away on the first try is lost.

The spider works all her spinnerets, each making a different kind of silk.

A garden spider with two insects trapped in its web.

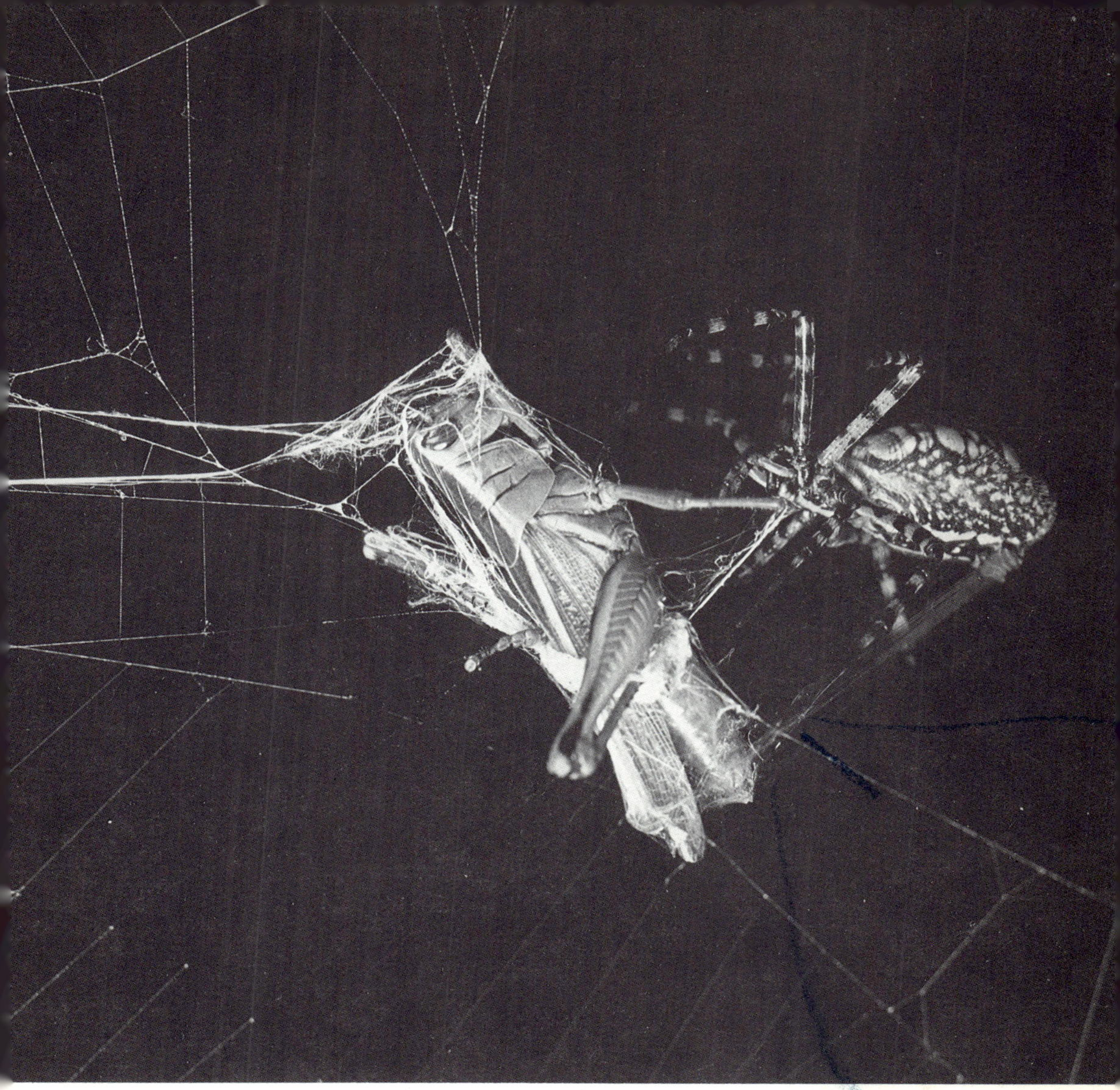

Wrapping up a captured grasshopper.

This crab spider is feeding on a moth.

Slowly the insect is covered by the silk.

It is tied, but not dead.

Spiders eat only live things.

The spider digs her fangs into the grasshopper.

The poison keeps the grasshopper from moving, but does not kill it.

The spider bites the grasshopper and sucks out all its juices.

The part that is left is pushed out of the web.

The spider goes back to the middle of the web.

WEBS OF ALL KINDS

Not all spinners are orb weavers.

The web pattern of each kind will change only during a strange happening.

Arabella and Anita, two garden spiders, took a trip in space.

Arabella's web spun on earth.

NASA

Arabella's web spun in a Skylab in space.

NASA

Nothing—not even you and I and spiders—weighs anything in space.

This is because there is no pull by the earth.

Scientists wanted to know how spiders would weave out in space.

A drug that gives people bad dreams changed the way a spider spun its web when the spider ate a fly that had been put in the drug first.

The disorganized web on the right was made after a spider had been fed an insect dipped in a drug.

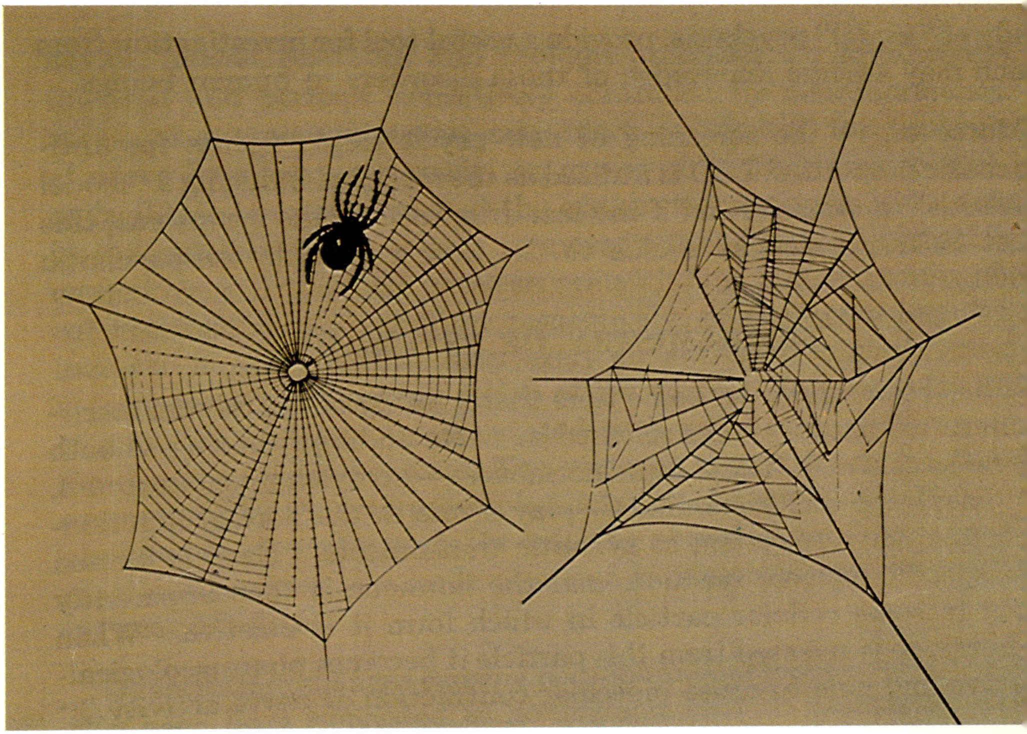

P. N. Witt

THE HUNTERS

Spiders that hunt jump on their food on the ground or in the air.

Some can see well and hunt in the day.

The **wolf spider** is so fierce a hunter that its name *Lycosa* (lie-KO-sah), in Greek, means "tearing like a wolf."

It runs fast and springs on its prey.

It holds it with its front legs.

Then it crushes the prey with its strong jaws.

A burrowing wolf spider in its hole.

A jumping spider

The **jumping spiders** jump for their food.
They hunt in the bright sun.
They can leap long distances to land on their prey.

They can even catch an insect when it is flying.

They can figure out very well how far they have to jump.

Yet before jumping they let out a dragline.

If they miss their mark, they can climb back on the dragline.

The jumping spider uses a "safety line" when jumping.

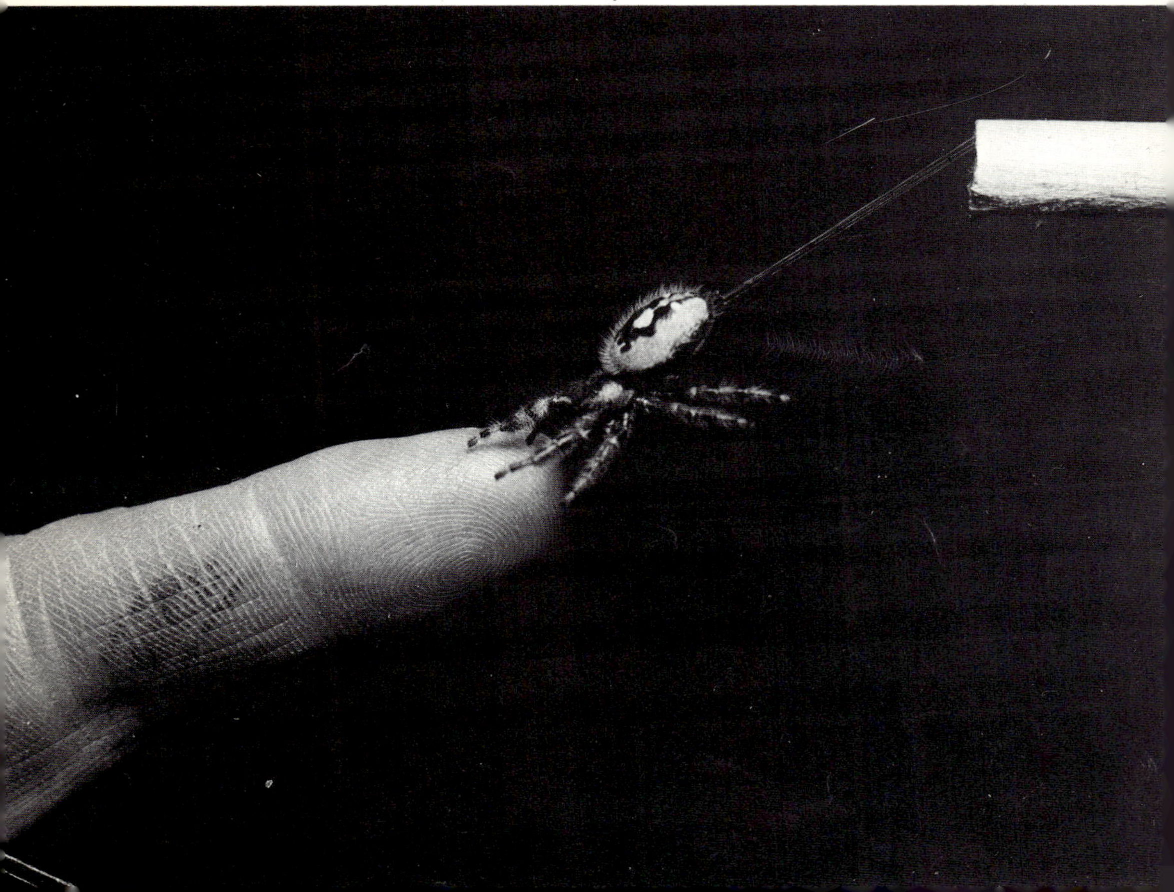

Crab spiders

The **crab spider** is another spider that goes out to hunt for food.

It holds its legs at its side and walks sideways like a crab.

A small one can win over a bee that is much larger and heavier.

Like the jumping spider it climbs up a dragline.

Crab spiders wait in hiding in flowers.

Some even change color while sitting on a flower.

Banana spiders

The **huntsman** or **banana spider** is over 1 inch (over 2.5 cm) long.

When its legs are stretched out, it can cover most of your hand.

It used to come to our country in bunches of bananas on ships.

Often when people saw it, they became frightened.

They thought it was a "poisonous tarantula" (tah-RANCH-a-lah).

These spiders can be tamed.

They like to eat cockroaches.

FISHING SPIDERS

A **fishing spider**, called a **raft spider** in England, moves along the top of the water.

Holding on to a water flower, it dives for food.

Bubbles caught on its body hairs give it air until it returns to land to eat.

Fishing spiders

A true **water spider** in Europe spins a partly round web filled with air. It carries the web under the water.

The spider swims upside down.

It eats water bugs.

A wolf spider carrying her young.

Some **wolf spiders** dig holes.

The **trap-door spider**, the best of the diggers, digs a tube 10 inches (25 cm) deep and 1½ inches (5.5 cm) across.

The female digs this nest.

She lines it with silk.

Next she builds a round lid.

It is a trapdoor.

She makes it stronger with another webbing of silk.

American Museum of Natural History

The nest of a trap door spider.

The **trap-door spider** hunts at night.

She can't see very well, but she seems to know when an insect is passing by.

She throws open the trapdoor, but keeps part of her body inside.

She must not be locked out of her home.

With one quick move she bites the prey with her fangs.

When that happens, the prey can't move.

Then the spider carries the prey into the hole.

THE POISONOUS ONES

Only two well-known kinds of spiders in North America are dangerously poisonous.

They are the **widows** and the **brown spiders**.

The **black widow** likes to live where it is warm.

The female is jet black.

Its belly has a red mark.

It is shaped like some bottles.

Only the female bites.

She bites into the skin with her tiny fangs.

The poison spreads and makes the person very, very sick.

The person must quickly get a special medicine to act against the poison.

A black widow hanging from a twig.

A brown recluse spider.

U.S.D.A.

The **brown recluse spider** hides in dark places around the house, such as behind chairs or in clothes that are hanging up or in beds.

A recluse is a person who likes to live alone.

That is why this spider is called the **brown recluse spider**.

Once there were very few **recluse spiders** in the United States.

Now it lives in many places, mostly in the South.

Its bite can make a person very, very sick.

THE GIANT IS NOT POISONOUS TO PEOPLE

The **tarantula**, a hairy, brown spider found in Brazil, is 3 inches (7.5 cm) long.

When its legs are stretched out, this giant among spiders may reach 10 inches (25 cm).

It feeds on birds and small snakes.

Its size and thick hair make people think it is poisonous.

A hairy tarantula, from South America.

A red and black tarantula, one of the most colorful of all spiders.

The **tarantulas** of the United States are smaller and do not move around as much as the ones of Brazil.

They live in holes in the ground and hunt at night.

Tarantulas are not very poisonous and may even be kept as pets.

They may live to be 25 years old.

That's old for a spider.

Most spiders only live a year or two.

To grow, a tarantula **molts**, or sheds its outer shell. It grows a bigger one each time this happens.

Some people keep tarantulas as pets.

This jumping spider waves his front legs to get his mate's attention.

TIME FOR BABIES

When the time comes to mate, the male looks for a female.

He may see a mate or feel one with his hair.

He taps the web in a special way.

This can be dangerous, and he has to watch his step.

He has to be sure the female wants him for a mate and not for food.

Some spiders bring a dead insect as a present.

If she takes it, he has found his mate.

At the tip of each of his pedipalps (PED-die-palpz) he carries a drop of sperm.

He places it in an opening in the female's abdomen.

After this, he soon dies, or a stronger spider or his mate may eat him.

Male and female black widows mating.

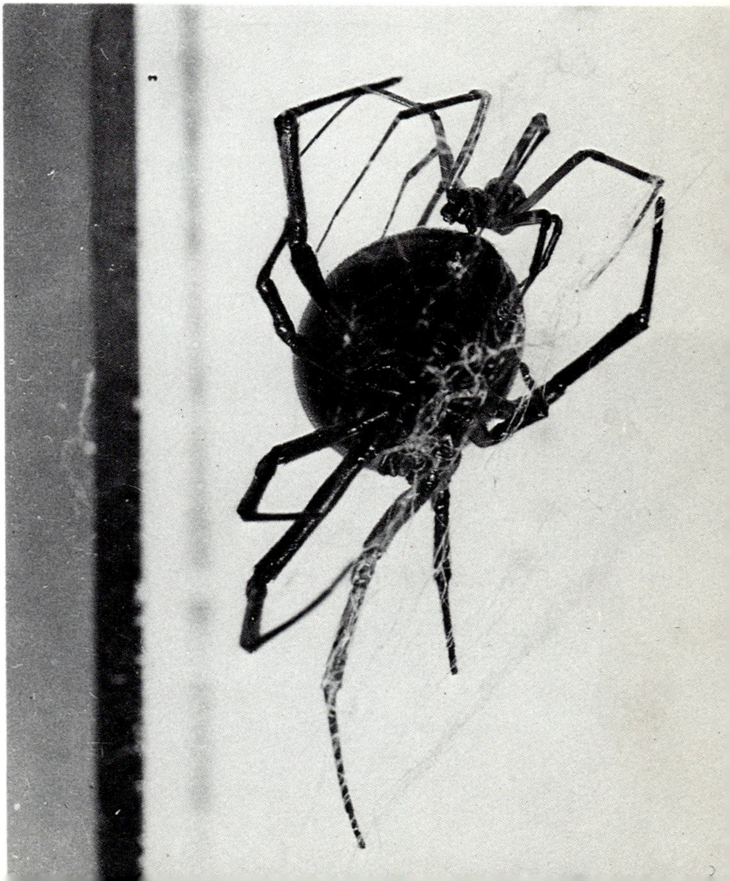

After mating, the female black widow traps her mate in her sticky webbing, and prepares for a meal.

Alone, mother spider raises her family.

She weaves a silken nest for her many eggs and keeps guard over them.

Weeks or even months later, the baby spiders, or **spiderlings**, as they are called, need her to protect them from wasps and birds.

The babies of some spiders go ballooning.

They let out lines of silk.

They then let go and are lifted into the air.

Any light wind carries them along like a balloon that has been let go.

After the spiderlings leave, the mother spider dies.

But her many young will grow. They too will have spiderlings in many places.

This is nature's way.

There will always be spiders in the world.

A garden spider guards her sac of eggs.

SPIDER ENEMIES

Frogs, lizards, birds, insects, and even other spiders are spiders' enemies.

Hunting spiders feed on spiderlings.

But wasps are the greatest enemy of spiders.

People kill spiders, too.

A jumping spider and a crab spider get ready to fight.

Spiders are an important form of animal life.

Dusting cobwebs through the house can kill spiders.

Farmers often spray fields to kill insects that eat plants.

This can also kill the spiders there.

A spider that has been stepped on can't kill insects that eat our food growing in the fields.

Remember, spiders are our good animal friends.

INDEX